Unheard Voices

A Mother's Hidden Diary

Anupama Venkatesh

BookLeaf Publishing

India | USA | UK

Made with ❤ on the BookLeaf Publishing Platform
www.bookleafpub.in
www.bookleafpub.com

Dedication

Dear Amma,

You are my guiding star,
My strength, my inspiration.
The superwoman I aspire to be,
The heart of my motivation.
With endless love and gratitude,
I dedicate this to you.

Preface

This collection is drawn from a hidden journal of my mother, a woman who embraced single parenthood long before life had fully unfolded. Like a tree weathering countless storm, *Unheard Voices –A Mother's Hidden Diary* captures her reflections through grief, joy, triumph, and quiet introspection.

These poems, written in solitude, carry the wisdom of her past and present experiences and the love she poured into raising two children alone. They are letters of strength, hope, and guidance—meant not just for us, but for anyone walking a similar path.

With deepest love and respect, I share these verses in the hope that they bring comfort to those navigating life's shadows. May they especially resonate with single mothers—the quiet heroes—and remind them of their strength and shared journey.

Acknowledgements

I am deeply grateful to my mother, Mrs. Anuradha V, who shared her heart's journal with me so openly and has been my greatest inspiration—as a woman, a writer, and a loving parent throughout my life.

To my family and siblings in special mention, thank you for being the unknowing muses behind my interest in writing poems. Your presence has always stirred something poetic in me.

To my friends from my workplace, your encouragement and unwavering support have been the quiet force behind all my endeavours.

A special thanks to my dear friend Mrs. Ruchi Ranade, for the time, energy, and thoughtful feedback you offered—and for being my cheerleader through every page of this book.

And finally, for my late father, with love, with longing, and with hope that these words bring you pride and peace.

A-Z of Life

Attempt to all work

Be prompt

Consider Well

Decide positively to do right

Endure trials patiently

Fear to do wrong and fight bravely in life

Goal is important in life

Hold to your goals tightly

Injure not others heart

Judge others' intention and act accordingly

Keep away all your evil thoughts

Lie not for any considerations

Make your acquaintances

Never try to appear as what you are not

Observe good things only

Pray god every day and every time

Question reasonably to whoever so whenever and wherever required

Respect those who are elder to you

Sacrifice is important but not your principles

Tolerance in certain things is necessary
Use your leisure for improvement
Venture not upon the wrong things
Watch your passions and your words
Xtend your hand for good causes
Yield not discouragement
Zealously labour for right

Lessons on Life

Life is a query, it is a mystery
Life is a boon, so thank him soon
Life is beautiful and full of duties
Life is joyful, so please take care
Life is a puzzle and may push you in the middle
Life is a beginning, & as each day unfolds, be bright and
bold
Life is a treasure, so explore without any pressure
Life is a book, so fill it with your unique story
Life is a journey, so embrace it with all your energy

It's all upto you my girl,
on how you desire it to furl and how you hurl.

Power of Words

Actions speak louder than words, but words hold a unique power as they instantly reach the hearts and minds. Actions Build, Words Heal- Both are essential forces

A careless word may kindle strife
A cruel word may wreck a life
A bitter word may hate in still
A brutal word may smile and kill
A gracious word may smooth the way
A joyous word may light the day
A timely word may lessen the stress
A loving word may heal and bless

Words of Life

The most bitter word- LONELINESS
The most revered word - MOTHER (AMMA)
The first earthly word - BIRTH
The last temporal word - DEATH
The cruel word - REVENGE
The peaceful word - HARMONY
The saddest word- FORGOTTEN
The warmest word- FRIENDSHIP
The coldest word - NO
The comforting word- TRUST
The fleeting word - TIME
The binding word - LOVE
The shattering word - LOSS
The radiant word - JOY
The haunting word - PAST
The whispered word - SECRET
The echoing word - FUTURE

Burden of Blunders

When a judge makes a mistake
It becomes a law
When a doctor makes a mistake
It becomes a new diagnosis
When an architect makes a mistake
It becomes a new design
when an educationalist makes a mistake
It becomes a new principle
When a scientist makes a mistake
It becomes a discovery

But I wonder,
When I make a mistake,
I hear the whispers of doubt,
A gentle nudge, yet still,
It feels like a weight I can't shake.
So, I try to hide away,
To be like those who excel,
Yearning to rise above,
But fearing the shadows that dwell.

A Smile goes a Mile

For all of us young or old
Those who may be timid or bold
One's character how-so-ever vile
Can be overcome by a single slight smile.

One may travel by road or rail
In certain attempts one my fail
Varying problems in one's heart may pile
Can be overcome by a single slight smile.

Today there may be changes in trends
Tomorrow foes may become friends
Success may be away by many a mile
Can be overcome by a single slight smile.

Smiling helps wining other's confidence
Sure its far more than a sage's penance
Modern or primitive may be your lifestyle
But the base of everything is to just smile.

Feel It All, Heal It All

Man is made of emotions,

Grief, joy, pain, laughter, anger, and fear

Some bring peace, while some bring commotion.

But all are yours to experience, Oh my dear!

Everything has to be felt

Despite the pain it brings

Because the feelings that aren't dealt

Turns to traumas that we cling

Let it all out, Feelings come first, without a doubt.

Hiding them doesn't mean that it's sent out

In some dark corner of our heart and mind,

Where dreams are hidden and hopes confined,

Just let it all unwind.

Cause justice delayed is justice denied.

Laughter and tears, both good for us,

Undergo them and set the spirits free

Moments of joy and times of big fuss

Perceive all and embrace what's meant to be.

Seize Today

What you think, act today
The time will pass, and thoughts change
What you want to achieve, win it today
Since the winners change
What you want to see, see It today
Because the scene change
What you want to accomplish, finish it today
As the end may never come

What you feel, embrace it today
For emotions shift, like tides in the bay
What you dream, believe it today
As dreams take flight, then often stray.
What you seek, pursue it today
For paths may twist, then lead you away.
What you love, cherish it today
Since love can fade,yet always stay.

Today is always the right time
To weave your moments, in rhythm and rhyme

My Man - Beyond Wedding Vows

I've always dreamt of a husband so dear,
With qualities that bring comfort and cheer.
These heartfelt wishes, simple and true,
and I hope I find solace while I grow
He should be a medicine, when am in pain
He should be my letter, when am far
He should be my smile when am sad
He should be my thoughts when am mad
He should be my step when I walk
He should be my hanky when I cry
He should be my life when I die.

The Balance

Amidst the darkness of deepest of fears,
Change arrives as a light called courage
Amidst the brightness of the deepest of joys
There emerges a shadow called freedom
Amidst the happiness of greatest of achievements
There is a rival called jealousy
Amidst the sorrow of worst of failures,
There is a ray of hope
Amidst the joy of greatest of victories
There is a lost friendship with pride
Amidst the circumstances of deepest of emotions
It is the "relationship with god"

A Letter to the Anchor of my Heart

You were a shoulder to lean on when I needed support
You appreciated even my slightest effort
You lent an empathetic hand when I suffered loss
You were the laughter, and a hug I needed when I cried
And you were the one I trusted myself completely.
Flowers around remind me your face
and the life I lived with you- my happy place
The morning sunrise reminds me your sparkling eyes
And the days you comfort me with your romantic lies
Beach waves sounds reminds me your rough voice
Enabling me to handle life with grace and poise
The sky above my head, reminds me that you are there
Leading me through all highs and lows with care
Oh, my love!
Roses can die, rivers can dry
People forget, but our heart
Though miles apart
My love and respect,
For you never departs.

Whispers of the Nights

When the night sets in,
Darkness takes the win.
Likewise in my empty distressed heart,
the unhealed voices lead the part
These unanswered echoes of past wounds
Buzz and fade around.
Pulling me down, and surrounding me in fear
Of helplessness, binding me over and over
Nights has always been peace
To people who have life at ease
But for me, it brings in deep fear
Of emptiness accompanied with long tears
Every night, I cry out loud,
With fear of being lost and unfound.
Thought of survival through this misery
will forever remain a mystery.
The nights remind me of my past scars.
And the deep wounds don't let me go any further
thereby raising a wild question,
Filling my eyes with tears, blurring my vision.

Is my life's destiny to be lonely?
A constant thought that lives hopelessly,
Thinking about that makes me insane,
Leaving pain as my only gain.
I am looking for an acceptance I have been wanting
Whispering powerful prayers day in and out, hoping
That the divine aura surrounding helps me out
From the dark, depressing, lonely thought.

Wealth of Time

Take time to read, it is the foundation of wisdom
Take time to think, it is the source of power
Take time to play, it is the secret to stay young
Take time to laugh, it is the music to soul
Take time to work, it is the price of success
Take time to pray, it is the greatest power on earth
Take time to serve people, it is the duty of every human
Take time to speculate, it is one of the secret progress
Take time to love, it is a bond that lasts forever
Take time to dream, it is a source of achievement
Take time to forgive, it is a way to unload worries
Take time to share, since life is short to be selfish

Perception of Life

In life,
If you can't come first, try not to come last
If no one is with you, be the someone with you
If you don't win, appreciate your participation
If nobody trusts you, try being your confidant.
If you can't rise, try not to stay
If shadows loom large, dance with the dark
If silence surrounds you, whisper your spark
If dreams seem distant, draw closer the light
If hope seems fleeting, hold on with all might.
So, cherish your path, no matter how it's paved

Painted Emptiness

A Work without sincerity
A worship without spirituality
A man without humanity
Love without divinity
Manners without dignity
People without hospitality
Poetry without originality
A life without morality
A Temple without a deity
And a Nation without integrity
Are nothing but echoes in the emptiness
Beautiful, yet meaningless.

Small Steps Forward- Mirror Talk

My Whole Life
From a girl to a man's wife,
Now feels like a blink —
When I sit and think.
My innocent eyes
Now bordered by dark circle pies.
My milky soft skin
Wrinkled now, as time's next of kin.
My always-running legs
Now crave rest and tender begs.
My long black hair —
Oh God, don't take me there.
My fairness and glow
Have dimmed, like the afterglow.
The young, energetic blood
Now panics at the slightest thud.
 So many thoughts have changed,
More I've gained — and more, I've drained.
But still — I rose, I remained.

Small Steps Forward-
Through the Storm

When I stepped out to see the light,
I was wed before the world felt right.
When I tried to know him, barely a clue,
I found I was pregnant before love even grew.

When I embraced love's sacred way,
Then watched my husband fade away.
When I sought my purpose, bold and wide,
But lost my job, my dreams denied.

When I began to heal my pain,
I was cast out in pouring rain.
When I rose to face each test,
My children were taken — "for their best."

When I worked late into the night,
They whispered names, devoid of light.
When I dared to see anew,
I was used by men, their hearts untrue.

They saw my body — a tempting art,
But never once looked at my heart.
But still — I rose, I remained.

Small Steps Forward- Miles of Hope

Some days, it was just me,
Alone in a house that was just a key.
Silence wrapped around the room,
Thick with heaviness and gloom.

Now, peace and silence feel divine,
But then, they were my prison's sign.
No key, no bail — just me and a weary tale.
There were days I begged for meals,
And starved through nights with silent squeals —

But then my child's warm smile
Would carry me another mile.

In the process, I refrained,
For love's sake, to keep it sustained.
But still — I rose, I remained.

Small Steps Forward- in the Hands of Time

I believe in the One above,
The almighty giver of silent love.
He threw me in, watched from afar —
But never let me truly fall apart.

This wasn't what I signed for,
But I've come far — and even more.
I'm proud to say I've nailed it,
Without a map, a guide, or a kit.

Life showed me in its strange ways
That these are merely passing days.
No matter the mood or the blues,
There's always something good to choose.

I've learned that life isn't always sought —
Sometimes, it just happens... or not.
But still — I rose, I remained.

Small steps Forward- Living a Life that Matters

Now, fifty years and countless tears,
I've learned through joy and hidden fears:

That only you should steer your hand.
That being selfish helps you stand.
Choosing joy once in a while
Is like adding a missing smile.
That your health is a precious treasure,
Not what the world wants you to hold.
That speaking up when silence bites
Is a right, not a fight.
That mourning loss won't move your feet —
You need to rise, not repeat.
That whatever happens — it's meant to be,
And through it all, choose to be free.
Now looking back, it wasn't a walk in the park.
But the lesson I take is real — not half-baked.
I didn't get the life I dreamt,
But I live a life that matters,

Held by faith when all else scattered.
With scars that speak, and strength unplanned,
I rise each time — by my own hand.

Growing Stronger

There's a saying that's true: the older the wine,
The richer its taste, the deeper its shine.
That goes the same with our life's travel—
The more we walk through dust and gravel,
The more we heal, the more we unravel.

Once, I cared for the trendy dress,
Chased the glow, the outward finesse.
But now I value peace and rest—
A mind that's calm, a heart well-dressed.

Once, I lived through others' eyes,
Did good deeds just to win the prize.
Now I've stepped into my lead,
Living a life that I truly need.

Once, I feared what they might say,
Held my truth and danced their way.
But now I twirl through voices that swirl,
Rooted and bold—no longer that girl.

I used to ignore my inner calls,
Wished for wings inside their walls.
Now I listen—loud and clear,
My voice is the one I hold most dear.

Once I thought I had to be rough,
To prove I'm strong, to feel enough.
But now I know, in every test,
I've always held the strength to rest

.

Once I lived to help, to mend,
Even when my own would bend.
But now I've learned to softly grip,
Let go of guilt and the endless trip.

I once believed that dreams come true,
Only when wished on skies so blue.
But now I see—I am the dream,
Shaped through every scar and seam.

Once, I didn't know how to act untold
How to bloom in this spinning world.
Still, I don't know all that's right—
But I know I'll pass with time that doesn't wait.